Editor
Amethyst W. Gaidelis, M.A.

Editor in Chief
Karen J. Goldfluss, M.S. Ed.

Illustrator
Kelly McMahon

Cover Artist
Tony Carrillo

Art Coordinator
Renée McElwee

Imaging
James Edward Grace
Craig Gunnell

Publisher
Mary D. Smith, M.S. Ed.

TCR 3974

S0-AGA-175

DAILY WARM-UPS

Grade **1**

Nonfiction & Fiction

Writing

Includes:

➤ *150 writing activities that target six writing traits*

➤ *engaging nonfiction and fiction writing topics*

➤ *writing prompts for additional practice*

➤ *standards and benchmarks*

Ideas and Content
Word Choice
Fluency
Voice
Organization
Conventions

Focused, fun writing practice every day!

Teacher Created Resources

Author

Ruth Foster, M. Ed.

Teacher Created Resources
6421 Industry Way
Westminster, CA 92683
www.teachercreated.com
ISBN: 978-1-4206-3974-2
© *2012 Teacher Created Resources*
Made in U.S.A.

Teacher Created Resources

Table of Contents

Introduction

The written word is a valuable and mighty tool. It allows us to communicate ideas, thoughts, feelings, and information. As with using any tool, skill comes with practice. *Daily Warm-Ups: Nonfiction and Fiction Writing* uses high-interest, grade-level-appropriate exercises to help develop confident, skillful writers.

This book is divided into seven sections. Each of the first six sections focuses on one of the following key writing traits. These traits have been identified by teachers as effective tools for improving student writing. The last section in the book offers a set of writing prompts to encourage further writing opportunities throughout the year.

Nonfiction and Fiction—Writing Traits Focus

IDEAS and CONTENT   **VOICE**

WORD CHOICE   **ORGANIZATION**

FLUENCY   **CONVENTIONS**

Daily Warm-Ups: Nonfiction and Fiction Writing uses a format that allows for flexibility in both instruction and learning. You may wish to begin with Warm-Up 1 and progress sequentially through all or most of the writing practices provided in the book. As an alternative, begin by introducing and modeling a specific writing trait that needs to be addressed. Students can then use the warm-ups within that section to practice and apply the trait as they complete each of the writing activities. Once the section is completed, continue working through the remaining sections based on the needs of the class.

With 150 independent warm-ups, there are plenty of writing opportunities to last the entire school year. As with any subject to be learned and mastered, writing should be continually practiced. With an arsenal of good writing techniques and an understanding of the writing process at their disposal, students can achieve a comfort level regardless of the writing task. Daily writing and guided practice using essential writing traits can help students reach a measurable level of success.

The activities in this book were designed to help students gain experience writing in response to both nonfiction and fiction prompts. Each topic or theme includes pages that address both fiction and nonfiction writing.

> The warm-up activities allow students to use both nonfiction and fiction writing on the same topic!

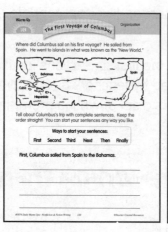

These paired warm-ups are about giving directions. The first warm-up presents nonfiction information and asks the writer to describe the steps of a historic journey using the facts and tips provided.

The second warm-up introduces the same skill in the form of a scenario and requires the student to give directions to a treasure, while still practicing organizing steps with transitions.

The writing exercises in this book give students the opportunity to use a variety of writing formats. This allows a student to practice a specific writing skill while developing an understanding that good writing traits can be incorporated into a number of genres. The variation also keeps the daily writing activities exciting.

Each of the first six sections contains 25 warm-up writing pages that focus on the specific trait featured in the section.

The activities are written so that all students in a class can participate. While highly competent students may write more complex responses, all students will be able to practice writing at their respective levels of competence on a daily basis.

Each section ends with a page that incorporates both nonfiction and fiction writing activities. This page can be used as a culminating activity for the section, or as an informal assessment representative of the student's writing using the specific writing trait.

Space has been provided for students to write their responses on the activity page. For instances in which students need additional space to complete an activity, they can use the back of the page or continue on separate paper. Encourage students to use notebooks where they can extend their writing or create new writing pieces if they choose to do so.

The last section of the book includes a set of writing prompts that can be used throughout the year. These provide ideas, story starters, and a variety of scenarios for students to use as prompts. Students (or the teacher) can select one prompt a week to use as a topic for their writing. As an alternative, select a prompt and ask students to focus on one or two specific traits as they write. There are many ways to use these prompts. Choose a method that works best for you and your students.

Good Writing Traits

Ideas and Content

This trait lays the foundation for other aspects of effective student writing. Students need to learn to develop and organize their ideas and present them clearly. Students should gather their ideas, as well as research, seek new knowledge, and organize their information, before they begin to write. Successful writers write about what they know, the subjects in which they have expertise, or specific knowledge and experience.

In practicing the characteristics of this trait, students identify topics about which they have prior knowledge, investigate and explore topics further by conducting additional research if needed, and learn to connect their writing to their own experiences.

Writing that is strong in content includes interesting, relevant, specific details and a development of the piece as a whole. Students should have opportunities to practice organizing their ideas, writing about their own experiences, using examples and details, and writing complete pieces. This allows them to use insight and understanding to show readers what they know.

Word Choice

Paying attention to word choice enables students to write effectively so the reader will understand and want to read. Elements of the word-choice trait include using strong visual imagery and descriptive writing.

Writers learn to use accurate and precise words to say exactly what they want to communicate. Specific words convey distinct meanings. Students should use action words, as well as descriptive nouns and adjectives, to give their writing energy.

Using effective word choice implies a familiarity with the language as students learn to use parts of speech and subject-verb agreement properly. An effective writer listens to how words sound, using words that sound natural and add to the meaning of the writing.

As students become more adept at choosing the right words to express their intent, their written communication will be more easily understood and enjoyable to read.

Fluency

As students learn to incorporate the trait of fluency in their writing, they should continue to practice what they learned about the word-choice trait. As writers develop fluency, they play with different word patterns and use words to match the mood of their writing. Fluent writing contains sentences varying in length and structure.

Students should learn to express themselves in clear sentences that make sense. This will happen as they incorporate natural rhythm and flow in their writing, making sure that ideas begin purposefully and connect to one another.

A writer may engage in a process of thinking that begins by asking the question, "What if?" One question leads to another, and the writer begins to develop smooth transitions and pacing. Mastery of each component of the fluency trait leads to a final outcome—the ability to pass a "read-aloud" test.

As students learn about the fluency trait, they should practice ways to express themselves by writing in a variety of formats. They will gather words to create word patterns and match specific moods.

Good Writing Traits *(cont.)*

Voice

As students gain confidence using the trait of fluency, they begin to learn about writing style. The voice trait focuses specifically on a writer's individual style. An effective piece of writing that exhibits aspects of the voice trait will sound like a particular person wrote it. Therefore, writing that has characteristics of voice will also be fluent; it will have natural rhythm. Authors develop their own unique style by writing from their thoughts and feelings. An author's personality comes through in his or her writing. Effective writers focus on their audience: They write to the reader. They want to call attention to the writing and draw the reader in. To do this, authors will write honestly, sincerely, and with confidence. As they write based on their own experiences and knowledge of themselves, writers will have the ability to bring a topic to life.

Students should continue to practice expanding their perspectives, as well as read sample pieces written from another person's point of view. By doing so, they will learn to identify elements of the voice trait in written samples and begin to develop their own style by writing reflections and personal correspondence.

Organization

Once students learn to incorporate the organization trait in their writing, they begin to view the whole picture. Effective writing has a logical order and sequence with clear direction and purpose; it does not confuse the reader. Rather, writing that displays qualities of organization guides the reader through the writing, leading to the main point. Writers who incorporate the characteristics of the organization trait include an introduction that captures the reader's attention and conclude the piece by making the reader think. Organized writing flows smoothly, with transitions that tie together.

Students can practice the characteristics of this trait by learning about beginnings and endings of stories and paragraph structure. They should practice writing their own paragraphs. The teacher can assist by introducing story elements to the students and giving them opportunities to outline a story, identify story elements, and write a complete story. As students learn to organize their written work, they begin to focus on appropriate pacing and transitions in their writing, leading to a more cohesive and readable final product.

Conventions

Students put the pieces together as they worked through the organization trait and began to consider the whole picture. They also had opportunities to consider self-evaluation, based on established criteria. The next major step in the writing process is editing. The conventions trait breaks the huge task of editing into smaller parts—allowing students to practice editing their own and others' work, focusing on one factor at a time.

Students learn about and practice correct forms of conventions, such as correctly spelling plural and singular forms of nouns, capitalization of place names, punctuation, possessives, and subject-verb agreement. While students often practice characteristics of the conventions trait by reading and editing samples written by others, it is important that they continually edit their own work.

#3974 Daily Warm-Ups: Nonfiction & Fiction Writing   6   ©*Teacher Created Resources*

Presentation

The trait of presentation refers to the publication part of the writing process. After students have completed a written piece, they present it to their audience: visually, orally, or using both formats.

Students consider appropriate visual formats for their writing, as well as the use of color. Visual aids include charts, diagrams, and graphs. The visuals may include text. Specifically, students learn how to create a graph for a presentation.

The auditory component of presentation includes presenting work in an oral format; students learn public-speaking skills through drama and critique. Practicing this trait also gives students the opportunity to speak about a personal experience, ask and respond to questions, and clearly state their main point when presenting their writing to others.

 **A NOTE ABOUT PRESENTATION**

While presentation is not included among the sections of this book, its importance should not be discounted. The goal of the activities in this book is to provide relatively short, daily warm-up practice. The presentation process involves additional time and preparation. However, you can periodically allow students to display and present some of their writing to an audience with a focus on good visual and auditory techniques.

EVALUATING THE EFFECTIVE USE OF TRAITS IN THE WRITING WARM-UPS

As students work toward mastery of the writing traits and practice using them in their daily writing, it is important to assess their progress along the way. This can be done throughout the year. To determine whether a student is applying a trait to a particular writing piece, you may choose to evaluate the writing sample using a scoring rubric. Select those writing samples you wish to assess, and use one or more of the applicable writing traits to determine how well the student met the criteria.

A sample scoring rubric is provided on page 8. Each trait can be presented individually so that it can be used to help students as they first learn about the Good Writing Traits, or page 8 can be passed out in its entirety to serve as a reference.

Use each trait rubric by itself to score writing from that section or combine traits to match special assignments. You can also teach the traits in a cumulative manner, adding one trait to your rubric as you begin each section. Another option is to create your own descriptions using the blank rubric on page 9, following the example on page 8. Yet another alternative is to include students in the process by creating a rubric with them based on their growing understanding of each trait.

Before using any rubric, make sure students are aware of the criteria for which they will be assessed. Model sample writing pieces using the trait and criteria prior to using the rubric as a tool for evaluation. Keep in mind that a rubric is flexible and can be adapted for specific writing practice or group warm-ups. It is an effective and relatively quick way to assess student progress.

Sample Scoring Rubric

	4	3	2	1
Ideas and Content	The writing has a clear idea and the details support it well.	The writing has a clear idea and has relevant details.	The writing has a clear idea.	There is not a clear idea.
Word Choice	The writer carefully chose the best words based on the type of writing and the purpose.	The words are used correctly, but are not always the best choices.	One or two words are used incorrectly, or the vocabulary is limited.	Several words are used incorrectly, or there are not enough words used to show the meaning.
Fluency	Sentences flow easily and are a pleasure to read aloud. Different lengths and types of sentences are used to keep the writing fresh.	Most sentences flow well and are a pleasure to read aloud. There is some sentence variation.	The writing can be read aloud, but does not flow well.	The writing can only be read aloud with difficulty.
Voice	The writing is engaging and was written to a specific audience.	The writing was written to a specific audience.	The writing is generic. It is hard to tell what audience it was written to.	The writing is not engaging or appropriate for its audience.
Organization	The writing is clearly organized in a way that fits the purpose well.	The writing is clearly organized, and in most cases, includes an introduction, body, and conclusion.	The writing is organized in some way but the structure needs more work.	The writing has no structure. Events and information are random.
Conventions	The writing has correct spelling, punctuation, and capitalization.	The writing has mostly correct spelling, punctuation, and capitalization.	The writer has done some editing, but there are still many errors.	No editing has been done. Errors make the writing difficult to read.
Presentation	The writing is neat, and drawings, designs, or charts add appeal. If read aloud, it is easy to follow and it is clear the reader has practiced.	The writing is neat. The writer has added a drawing, design, or chart, or has prepared to read it aloud.	The writing is somewhat neat. If read aloud, it is read clearly.	The writing is messy. If read aloud, it is difficult to follow.

Sample Scoring Rubric

	4	3	2	1
Ideas and Content				
Word Choice				
Fluency				
Voice				
Organization				
Conventions				
Presentation				

Standards for Writing

Each activity in *Daily Warm-Ups: Nonfiction & Fiction Writing* meets at least one of the following standards and benchmarks, which are used with permission from McREL. Copyright 2012 McREL. Mid-continent Research for Education and Learning, 4601 DTC Boulevard, Suite 500, Denver, Colorado 80237. Telephone: 303-337-0990. Website: *www.mcrel.org/standards-benchmarks*.

To align McREL Standards to the Common Core Standards, go to *www.mcrel.org*.

1. **Uses the general skills and strategies of the writing process**

   - Prewriting: Uses prewriting strategies to plan written work

   - Editing and Publishing: Uses strategies to edit written work (e.g., edits for grammar, punctuation, capitalization, and spelling at a developmentally appropriate level; shares finished product)

   - Uses strategies to organize written work (e.g., includes a beginning, middle, and ending; uses a sequence of events)

   - Uses writing and other methods (e.g., using letters or phonetically spelled words, making lists) to describe familiar persons, places, objects, or experiences

   - Writes in a variety of forms or genres (e.g., letters, stories, poems, information pieces, invitations, personal experience narratives, messages, responses to literature)

2. **Uses the stylistic and rhetorical aspects of writing**

   - Uses descriptive words to convey basic ideas

3. **Uses grammatical and mechanical conventions in written compositions**

   - Uses conventions of print in writing (e.g., forms letters in print, uses upper- and lowercase letters of the alphabet, spaces words and sentences, writes from left-to-right and top-to-bottom, includes margins)

   - Uses complete sentences in written compositions

   - Uses nouns in written compositions (e.g., nouns for simple objects, family members, community workers, and categories)

   - Uses verbs in written compositions (e.g., verbs for a variety of situations, action words)

   - Uses adjectives in written compositions (e.g., uses descriptive words)

   - Uses adverbs in written compositions (e.g., uses words that answer how, when, where, and why questions)

   - Uses conventions of spelling in written compositions (e.g., spells high frequency, commonly misspelled words from appropriate grade-level list; spells phonetically regular words; uses letter-sound relationships)

   - Uses conventions of capitalization in written compositions (e.g., first and last names, first word of a sentence)

   - Uses conventions of punctuation in written compositions (e.g., uses periods after declarative sentences, uses question marks after interrogative sentences, uses commas in a series of words)

4. **Gathers and uses information for research purposes**

   - Researches topics of personal interest (e.g., generates questions about a topic)

Ideas
and
Content

The Giraffe

What do you know about giraffes?

Do giraffes have spots or stripes?

    Giraffes have _____ .

Do giraffes have four legs or six legs?

    Giraffes have _____ .

You can read more
about giraffes in books.

A giraffe's tail is very
long. It can be six
feet long.

Complete the sentences.

    I am _____ than a giraffe's tail!
                (taller/shorter)

    I have _____ legs than a giraffe!
                (more/fewer)

You can write about other animals, too. Write the name of each
animal in the correct box.

    tiger   cheetah   zebra   giraffe

Animals With Spots	Animals With Stripes

A Linny

You can write about a linny. A linny is not real. A linny is a made-up animal.

Does a linny have spots? Does a linny have stripes? Is a linny tall or short? You are the writer, so you choose what a linny looks like.

Complete the sentences.

My linny's name is _____ .

My linny _____ spots.

(has/does not have)

My linny _____ stripes.

(has/does not have)

I am _____ than my linny.

(taller/shorter)

Write another sentence or two about your linny. Draw a picture of it on the back of this paper.

_____

_____

_____

_____

_____

All About You

3

You can write about what you know. You know all about you.

My name is _____ .

I have _____ **hair.**
(short/long)

My hair is _____ .
(dark/light)

My eyes are _____ .
(brown/blue/green)

Look around you. Who else is like you? Complete the sentences.

_____ **has**

_____ **hair, too.**

_____ **has**

_____ **eyes, too.**

◆◆◆◆◆◆◆◆◆◆◆◆◆◆◆◆◆◆

You know more about yourself than what you look like. You know about things people cannot see. You know what you like to eat. You know what you like to do. Write down a thing that you like to do that people cannot tell by looking at you.
Complete the sentence.

I like to _____

_____

My Friend

You can write about someone you make up. Make up a friend. Your friend is not real. Your friend is in a story. You can make your friend any way you like.

My friend's name is _____ .

My friend has _____ **hair.**
(short/long)

My friend's hair is _____ .
(dark/light)

My friend's eyes are _____ .
(brown/blue/green)

◆◆◆◆◆◆◆◆◆◆◆◆◆◆◆◆◆◆◆

You are the writer. You choose what your friend likes to eat. You pick what your friend likes to do.

Write two sentences telling more about your friend. Draw a picture of your friend on the back of this paper.

My friend likes to _____

_____

_____

_____

How to Smile

You can write to tell people how to do the things you can do.

Can you write to tell people how to make a smile?

Think about what to write!

◆ Should the corners of your mouth be up or down?

◆ Do people usually show their teeth when they smile?

◆ How does your face look when you smile?

Write about what you think!

Use your ideas to tell people how to make a smile.

_____

_____

_____

_____

_____

_____

Happy Ways

You know many things. Use what you know when you are writing.

Draw a line from each animal or person to the thing it does to show it is happy.

cat	smiles
child	wags tail
dog	purrs

Think of an imaginary dog or cat. Imagine that it does not know how to show it is happy. What else can it do to show it is happy?

Now, write about the dog or cat.

Make up a name. _____

Tell what it looks like. _____

Tell what it does to show it is happy. _____

_____

Is there a time the dog or cat surprises people?

_____

_____

_____

Space Log

A log is like a journal. It is like a diary. People write down what happens in a log. They write down when and where things happen.

> ## Example
>
> Space Log: Neil Armstrong
>
> When: July 20, 1969
>
> Where: The Moon
>
> What: The first person walked on the Moon today.

Make your own log by using the information below.

November 3, 1957

The first Earthling went into space today.

The Earthling was a dog named Laika.

In space, Laika went around the Earth.

Space Log: _____
(your name)

When: _____

Where: _____

Who: _____

What: _____

The Astronaut's Log

No Earthling has gone to another planet. Pick a planet to go to. Think of some things you might see. Think of an adventure you might have.

Fill in the log with information about what you see and what you do.

Space Log: _____
(your name)

When: _____

Where: _____

What: _____

_____

Add to your log. Pretend you meet a creature from the planet you are visiting. Write down things about who you met.

_____

_____

_____

Now draw a picture of the creature on the back of this paper.

Some crabs were in danger. They had to cross a road to migrate. Too many cars were on the road. Crossing guards were needed. The guards were hired to help the crabs safely cross the road.

◆◆◆◆◆◆◆◆◆◆◆◆◆◆◆◆◆

Complete the ad for a crossing guard. Think about what you know about crabs when you write your answers!

Crossing Guard Wanted!

Where: _____

What you will do: _____

_____

What you should wear: _____

_____

What kind of person we will hire: _____

_____

_____

Smoke Jumper

You are a fire captain. You are hiring smoke jumpers. Smoke jumpers jump out of planes. They fight fires where there are no roads.

Complete the ad for a smoke jumper.

Smoke Jumper Wanted!

Wanted: _____

Where: _____

What you will do: _____

_____

What kind of person we will hire: _____

_____

Now write a sentence from someone who wants the job. The sentence should tell the captain why this person should be hired.

_____

_____

_____

Hot-Water Monkeys

11

People write letters. They write about what they see and do.

Japan is a country. Monkeys live in Japan. It snows. The monkeys get cold. How do the monkeys get warm? They sit in water! The water is hot. It is from a hot spring.

Here is a letter from the person who saw the monkeys. Fill in the missing words. To complete the letter, tell if other people should go, too.

_____
(date)

Dear _____ ,

I went on a trip to _____.

While I was there, I saw _____

_____

_____

_____

Sincerely,

_____

A Special Thing

You know a lot about where you live. Write a letter to someone who is not from where you live.

First, tell them where you live. Then, tell them something special about the place where you live. It may be a thing to do. It may be something to see. It may be an event that happens.

_____
(date)

Dear _____ ,

I live in _____ .

Where I live, _____

_____

_____

_____

_____

Sincerely,

_____

Someday

Someday you will be big. What will you be? You can be anything!

How can you know if you will like a job? You can read about it. You can ask workers about their jobs.

Think of what you might be one day. Write down why you think you might like that job. Then write down one question you would like to ask a person who does that job.

Job: _____

Why: _____

_____

_____

Question:

_____

_____

_____

_____

The Tadpole

A baby tadpole says, "Someday, I will be a big tadpole. I want to ask big, old tadpoles about their jobs. Why can't I find any big, old tadpoles to ask?"

Pretend you are a frog. Write down what you will say to the baby tadpole.

There are no old tadpoles because _____

_____ .

My job as a frog is to _____

_____ .

I like being a frog because _____

_____

_____

Anteater Facts

Writers need to check their facts. When giving information, they need to make sure what they write is true.

Decide if these sentences are true. Write **"True"** or **"False"**. Write why you think that. Use the Anteater Facts below.

You have fewer teeth than an anteater.

_____
(True/False)

Why? _____

_____

You have a shorter, narrower tongue than an anteater.

_____
(True/False)

Why? _____

_____

Anteater Facts

No teeth

Two-foot-long tongues

Tongues look like a strand of spaghetti

Anteater in the City

Write a story about an anteater that goes to the city. Write what might happen to the anteater when it tries to find or order food.

Use this fact in your story: *Anteaters eat up to 30,000 ants and termites a day.*

_____

_____

_____

_____

_____

_____

_____

_____

_____

A Rainy Place

17

You can find Mt. Waialeale in an atlas. Mt. Waialeale is in Kauai, Hawaii. It is one of the rainiest spots in the world. It rains over 450 inches a year on average. That is the same as 37.5 feet. It rains almost every day.

Think about the weather on Mt. Waialeale. Circle your choice.

On Mt. Waialeale, does it rain more feet than you are tall?

Yes   No

On Mt. Waialeale, does it rain more feet than your classroom wall is long?

Yes   No

Where you live, does it rain more or less than on Mt. Waialeale?

More   Less

How do you think it would be different to live on Mt. Waialeale?

_____

_____

_____

_____

The Flood

Pretend that it rains and rains where you live. Write a story about what happens when it rains very hard for many days.

When you write your story, think about a time when you have been out in the rain.

◆ What will you do?

◆ Where will you go?

◆ How will you get around?

◆ What exciting adventures will you have?

_____

_____

_____

_____

_____

_____

_____

_____

Think of your kitchen. How can someone tell your kitchen from someone else's kitchen? Make a picture with words. Write down details about your kitchen. The details should help someone picture your kitchen.

Use words from the Word Bank below to tell what you are writing about. Then finish each sentence with details.

> **Example**
>
> In my kitchen, the chairs are brown and have flowers painted on them.

In my kitchen, the _____

is _____.

The _____ is _____.

My kitchen is also different because the _____

is _____.

_____

_____

Word Bank	
refrigerator	cabinet
stove	chair
table	counter

Whose Living Room?

Pretend that you were sleepwalking. You woke up in a living room. There was a problem. The living room wasn't your living room!

Write down how you knew you were in the wrong living room. How is this room different? Use details about your own living room in the story.

This isn't my living room! In my living room, the _____

is _____. **Here, it is** _____ .

Also, _____

_____

_____

_____

_____

Word Bank	
couch	window
coffee table	curtains
lamp	carpet

Tiger!

It is important to use details that stick to the topic when you write. You are going to write about a tiger.

Cross out the details that do not stick to the topic.

A tiger

has stripes   pumpkins are orange

can swim   has sharp claws

is orange, black, and white   eagles have sharp claws

keeps claws sharp by pulling in when walking

This list is not complete. Write down two more details. The first detail should be about a tiger. The second detail should not stick to the topic.

Topic detail:

_____

_____

Detail that does not stick to the topic:

_____

_____

Trip to the Zoo

You want to make up a story about a trip to the zoo. Use details that stick to the topic.

Write down some details you might use in your story.

Who the story is about: _____

When the story takes place: _____

What animals are seen: _____

_____

Funny or interesting things done or seen:

_____

_____

_____

Now you can tell your story to someone or write it down on the back of this page. Include some of the details you wrote down.

What Do You Say?

People use examples when they write. An example is like a sample. It shows what something is like.

When do you say **"please"**? When do you say **"thank you"**? Write down two examples from your own life.

I say "please" when _____

_____.

For example, _____

_____

_____.

I say "thank you" when _____

_____.

For example, _____

_____

_____.

The Hungry Gorilla

Sam was eating a sandwich in his kitchen. A hungry gorilla came in without knocking. The hungry gorilla grabbed the sandwich. He ate it with his mouth open. Then he burped.

◆◆◆◆◆◆◆◆◆◆◆◆◆◆◆◆

Teach readers how to be polite. Use the gorilla as an example. Rewrite the story above. This time, correct all the things the gorilla does wrong. Write your new story.

The Polite Hungry Gorilla

Sam was eating a sandwich in his kitchen. A hungry gorilla

_____

_____

_____

_____

_____

Name Poem

There are many kinds of poems. There is a kind of poem called a name poem. To write a name poem, you write the letters of a word in a column. Then write a word or phrase that begins with each letter.

Example

Cat
Curious
A mouse catcher
Talks by purring

Write a name poem using the letters of your name.

First write the letters of your name in the boxes. Then think of a word or phrase that begins with the same letter as each letter in your name and tells something about you.

_____
(title — your name)

Word Choice

Cold or Freezing?

If something is **cool, cold**, or **freezing**, we know it is not hot. Still, a writer can decide how to make the reader feel by choosing cool, cold, or freezing.

Write down the most likely water temperature.

1. **Water with penguins:** _____.
   (cool/cold/freezing)

2. **Water in a swimming pool:** _____.
   (cool/cold/freezing)

3. **Water in a lake:** _____.
   (cool/cold/freezing)

Write a sentence or two telling about a time that you were cool, cold, or freezing. Think about what word you will use (cool, cold, or freezing).

_____

_____

_____

_____

_____

_____

Warm or Hot?

If something is **warm**, **hot**, or **burning**, we know it is not cold. Still, a writer can decide how to make the reader feel by choosing warm, hot, or burning.

Write down how someone might feel.

1. **Playing soccer on a summer day:** _____.
   (warm/hot/burning)

2. **Walking in a desert in the afternoon:** _____.
   (warm/hot/burning)

3. **In bed under a blanket:** _____.
   (warm/hot/burning)

Make up a story about a penguin who feels as if it is burning up.

Tell where the penguin is. Tell why it feels as if it is burning up. Do the people or other animals around the penguin feel as if they are burning up?

_____

_____

_____

_____

_____

_____

You can write about yesterday. Yesterday is in the past. Yesterday is over. You let your reader know you are writing about the past by using the right words.

Draw a line from each word to a phrase that fits.

yesterday	I run
yesterday	I ran
today	I saw
today	I see

Write what you had for breakfast, lunch, and dinner yesterday. Decide if you will use the word **eat** or the word **ate**.

Yesterday, I _____

_____ for breakfast.

Yesterday, I _____

_____ for lunch.

Yesterday, I _____

_____ for dinner.

You can write about tomorrow. Tomorrow is in the future. Tomorrow has not happened yet. You let your reader know you are writing about the future by using the right words.

Draw a line from each word to a phrase that fits.

tomorrow	I will fly
tomorrow	I am flying
today	I am swimming
today	I will swim

Write down what day of the week tomorrow will be.

Tomorrow will be _____ .

Now write one or two sentences telling what you will do tomorrow. Decide if you will use the word **will** or the word **am**.

_____

_____

_____

_____

_____

The Elephant

A boy and a girl have their eyes closed. The boy touches an elephant's leg. He says, "The elephant is like a tree trunk." The girl touches the elephant's trunk. She says, "The elephant is like a hose."

◆◆◆◆◆◆◆◆◆◆◆◆◆◆◆◆◆◆

Who is right? The boy and girl are both right! When you write, you can say things are like tree trunks and hoses. Your words help people picture what you are writing about.

Finish the sentences.

An elephant's tusk is like a _____ .

An elephant's tail is like a _____ .

Write your own sentence. Say what an elephant's ear or skin is like.

_____

_____

_____

_____

What Is It?

Write a riddle. Pretend your eyes are closed. You touch something. It can be an animal. It can be something you find in your bedroom or desk. Touch one part and say what it is like. Then touch another part and say what it is like. You can use words from the Word Bank below to help you.

My Riddle

I am touching something.

Its _____ is like _____.

Its _____ is like _____.

Its _____ is like _____.

What is it? It is a _____!

Word Bank

leg	paw	ear	mouth	tail	nose
top	bottom	side	tip	end	middle

You can read the first part of your riddle to the class. How many people knew the answer?

The Mountain

When you write, you use words to help readers make pictures in their heads. Adjectives are words that describe or tell about people, places, or things. An adjective might tell the color or size of something. An adjective might tell how something feels or tastes.

Which words could be adjectives? Circle the five adjectives.

red	big	dog	cat	small	striped	hot

Now it's your turn to think of adjectives.

Think of as many adjectives as you can to describe a mountain, a snake, your shirt, and a bus.

A mountain is	A snake is
My shirt is	**A bus is**

Story Plan

When you write a story, you can use adjectives to describe people, places, or things. Your adjectives help people make pictures in their heads when they are reading your story.

Plan a story. In your head, picture who the story is about. Picture where the story will take place. Write down all the adjectives you can about the characters and places in your story.

Name of character in story: _____

Adjectives: _____

Where the story takes place: _____

Adjectives: _____

Now use some of the adjectives you thought of in a sentence. In your sentence, describe who is in your story or where it takes place.

Examples

My story is about a soft, brown bunny.

My story takes place in a green, grassy park.

_____

_____

_____

Title Excitement!

Look at the story titles below. What story would you rather read?

1. **a. One Day**   **b. Fire on Ship!**

2. **a. Oldest Tree in the World**   **b. A Tree**

3. **a. Sleeping**   **b. Amazing Dream Leads to Invention**

When people write news stories, they try to make exciting titles. The exciting titles make people want to read or listen to the news stories.

Now it's your turn. Practice making titles that make people want to read more.

Old Title   **New Title**

1. Cat   _____

2. Safe   _____

3. The Game   _____

A Must-Read!

You own a bookstore. You want to sell lots of books. To sell more books, you put up a sign. The sign makes the book sound exciting.

Escape by a Hair!

Read how three little pigs were almost eaten by a big, bad wolf!

Think of a book, story, or nursery rhyme you have read. Write a sign about the story that makes people want to buy the book. Your sign should have a title and at least one sentence.

_____

_____

_____

_____

_____

Swimming with Penguins

Lynne Cox is a swimmer. She went to Antarctica. She swam in the icy water. She swam with the penguins. She liked swimming with the penguins.

◆◆◆◆◆◆◆◆◆◆◆◆◆◆◆◆◆

There is a wrong word in each sentence below. Write the correct word on the line.

Penguins swims in icy water. _____

Lynne Cox swim in icy water. _____

A writer needs to make sure each subject agrees with the verb. The subject is who or what the sentence is about. The verb is the action word.

Tell where your friend plays. Then tell where dolphins play. Decide if you will use the word **play** or **plays**.

My friend _____.

Dolphins _____.

Swimming with a Whale

One time Lynne Cox was swimming off the coast of California. A baby whale was lost. The baby whale started swimming with Lynne! Lynne swam with the baby whale until it found its mother.

◆◆◆◆◆◆◆◆◆◆◆◆◆◆◆◆◆◆

Pretend that you meet a baby whale while you are swimming. Complete three sentences about you and the whale. Make sure your subject agrees with your verb!

I _____

_____.

The whale _____

_____.

The whale and I _____

_____.

Writing to Whom?

We talk and write to different people in different ways. For example, you call your friends by their first names. You don't put **Miss** or **Mister** in front. You call your teacher and other adults by their last names. You put a **Mrs.**, **Ms.**, or **Mr.** in front.

Write **friend** or **adult** after each sentence to show who you are most likely writing to.

Hey, Jane, what's going on tomorrow? _____
(friend/adult)

Can you please help me tomorrow, Mrs. Woo?_____
(friend/adult)

In the box, write a sentence for each person. Be sure to include a name.

Friend
_____
_____
Teacher
_____
_____

The Visitor

You hear a knock on the door. You open it up and see a huge frog. The frog says, "I'm hungry."

Write down what you might say to the frog. You may or may not let the frog come in, but you want your words to be polite and respectful.

_____

_____

_____

_____

_____

_____

_____

_____

What's Buzzing?

You hear buzz, buzz, buzz. What animals might you be hearing?

dog	bee	cat	lion	mosquito	duck

1. _____

2. _____

Sometimes, writers want to include sound words. Sound words help the reader picture or feel a place. For example, you may be describing a garden. What sentence helps you most to picture the garden?

Bees flew from flower to flower.

Buzzing bees flew from flower to flower.

Write down all the sounds you can think of that the following animals might make:

duck _____

lion _____

owl _____

horse _____

On the Farm

Pretend that you have gone to a farm. Write several sentences that include all the sounds you might hear and what animals make them.

At the farm, I hear _____

_____

_____

_____

_____

_____

_____

What Animal?

Think of an animal. Write down three things about the animal. Then say what kind of animal it is.

Example

It has a mane.
It can roar.
It lives in Africa.
It is a lion.

Draw a picture of the animal.

The Talking Animal

In which story is the lion talking?

A. **It has a mane.**	B. **I have a mane.**
It can roar.	**I can roar.**
It lives in Africa.	**I live in Africa.**
It is a lion.	**I am a lion.**

The lion is talking in Story _____.

Lions can't talk in real life, but an author can make a lion talk in stories. Pretend you are an animal. Write down:

◆ something you have or how you look

◆ something you do

◆ where you live

Make sure to start your sentences with **I.**

_____

_____

_____

_____

A vet (veterinarian) is an animal doctor. One time, a rhinoceros had sore feet. The vet tried to help the rhino. The vet gave the rhino medicine, but it did not help. At last, the vet thought of something. It made the rhino shoes! The shoes were a bit like horseshoes. The shoes protected the rhino's feet.

◆◆◆◆◆◆◆◆◆◆◆◆◆◆◆◆◆◆◆

Think about what the vet was thinking when she saw the rhino. Write down what the vet might have thought while she treated the rhino. Start your sentences with the word **I**.

_____

_____

_____

_____

_____

_____

_____

The Rhino's View

A vet would not have the same thoughts as a rhino. When you are a writer, you can decide what a rhino might think and feel. Think about a rhino with sore feet. Think about how it felt before and after it got new shoes.

◆ Was it happy?

◆ Was it sad?

◆ Was it afraid?

◆ Did it know the vet wanted to help?

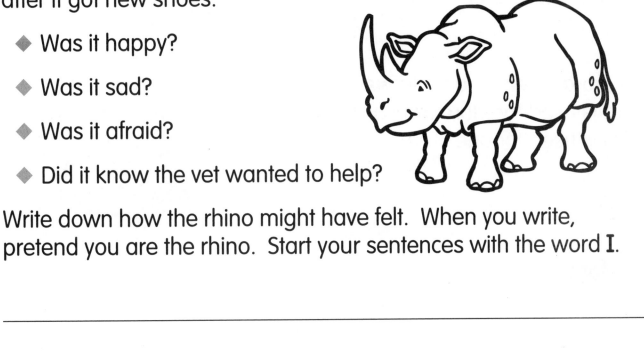

Write down how the rhino might have felt. When you write, pretend you are the rhino. Start your sentences with the word I.

_____

_____

_____

_____

_____

_____

Tooth or Teeth?

A shark has thousands of teeth. A shark's teeth are in rows. When one tooth falls out, one moves forward to take its place. A shark may lose thousands of teeth in its lifetime. Sometimes you can find shark teeth washed up on the shore.

◆◆◆◆◆◆◆◆◆◆◆◆◆◆◆◆◆◆

The words **teeth** and **tooth** were used in the story above. What word is used for more than one, and what word is used for one?

One: _____
          (tooth/teeth)

More than one: _____
                    (tooth/teeth)

Compare your teeth to a shark's teeth.

Do you have more or less? _____

How many teeth have you lost? _____

What do you do when you lose a tooth?

_____

_____

_____

How Many in a Week?

Sometimes you want to write about more than one thing. For most words, you add an **s** to make it plural (more than one).

Make each word plural.

1. book _____

2. dinosaur _____

3. eye _____

There are some plural words that do not follow this rule. See how many of these words you can make plural.

1. foot _____

2. tooth _____

3. mouse _____

What if you saw a mouse? The next day you saw a different mouse. Suppose you saw a different mouse every day for a week. At the end of the week, how many did you see?

Write a sentence telling how many you saw in a week.

In one week, I saw _____

_____

Different Places

The Atacama Desert is in Chile. It is very dry. It almost never rains. A little water comes from fog.

There are rainforests in Chile, too. In the rainforests, it rains a lot.

Picture in your head a desert and a rain forest. In the boxes, write down as many words as you can that describe each place.

Desert	Rainforest
_____	_____
_____	_____
_____	_____
_____	_____
_____	_____

Write a sentence telling what place you would rather visit and why. Then, on the back of this page, draw a picture of something you might find in one of the places. Make sure you write **desert** or **rainforest** above your picture.

_____

_____

How Do You Know?

 You go to sleep in a plane. You wake up, and you are in a new place. How do you know if you are in a desert? How do you know if you are in a rainforest?

You are the writer, so you can pick where you are. Write down how you know you are in a desert or a rainforest.

_____

_____

_____

_____

_____

_____

_____

_____

_____

Tongue Twisters

Read these tongue twisters. What beginning letter sound do you hear the most in each one?

Super silly Sally sells seashells at the sandy seashore.

Letter sound: _____

Peter Piper picked a peck of pickled peppers. If Peter Piper picked a peck of pickled peppers, where's the peck of pickled peppers Peter Piper picked?

Letter sound: _____

Tongue twisters are fun to hear and say. They can be hard to say. They can make you feel like your tongue is getting all twisted up!

Write a sentence that is fun to hear and say. You can write about something real or make something up. Try to make as many words have the same beginning letter sound as you can.

_____

_____

_____

Be ready to read your sentence out loud. Is it fun to say?

Fluency

What to Do with an Ear!

The man is <u>tall</u>.

He can jump the <u>wall</u>.

I have a <u>cat</u>.

It sees a <u>rat</u>!

The shark is <u>strong</u>.

Its tail is <u>long</u>.

What do you notice about the underlined words in each pair of sentences?

The words _____.

(rhyme/do not rhyme)

Complete the rhyming pair.

I have an ear. I use it to _____ .

Think of other rhyming pairs.

1. _____

_____

2. _____

_____

Jim the Kangaroo

I have a kangaroo named Jim.
Jim is slim.
Jim can jump over the basketball rim!

Sometimes writers use rhyming words to make their writing fun. You have read the rhyme about Jim. Now make up your own rhyme.

First, think of a thing you have. It can be an animal, pet, or friend. Write what you have and its name.

_____

Next, write some lines about your thing. Make sure the ends of your lines all rhyme.

_____

_____

_____

_____

When you are done, be ready to say your rhyme out loud. Is it fun to read and listen to?

Is it Yucky?

A spider has eight legs. Most spiders have eight eyes. Some people like spiders. They think spiders' legs and eyes are **wonderful**. Other people do not like spiders. They think they are **yucky**.

Think about the words someone might use to talk about a spider. Write down the words in the correct box.

Likes Spiders	Doesn't Like Spiders
_____	_____
_____	_____
_____	_____
_____	_____
_____	_____

Write a sentence telling what you think or feel about spiders.

_____

_____

_____

Now draw a picture of a spider on the back of this page. How many legs and eyes will your spider have?

The Grasshopper

A grasshopper is not a spider. A grasshopper is a kind of insect. Grasshoppers, like all insects, have six legs. Grasshoppers have five eyes.

Imagine that a grasshopper hops onto your foot. Think about what words will describe how you feel. Write them in the box.

Write a sentence or two telling how you feel about the grasshopper and why.

_____

_____

_____

_____

Now draw a picture of a grasshopper on the back of this page. How many legs and eyes will your grasshopper have?

What Weather?

It can snow. It can rain.

The wind can blow. The sun can shine.
People talk about the weather all the time.

Write a dialogue about the weather. A
dialogue is a conversation between two
people.

When you write, show who is talking by using a colon (:) after the
person's name. This is what people sometimes do when they are
writing plays.

Example

Max: It is going to snow tomorrow.
Megan: That is bad! I do not like the snow!

When you make up a dialogue, you get to decide how the weather
is. In your dialogue, ask someone what the weather will be like
tomorrow. What does the other person say? Do you like that kind
of weather? Tell why you are glad or sad about the weather.

_____ : _____
(Your name)

_____ : _____

_____ : _____
(Your name)

_____ : _____

Can you and a classmate read your dialogue out loud to the class?

Raining Ice Cream

Imaginary weather can be very strange! Pretend that it is raining ice cream! Is that good or bad? What might happen?

Write a dialogue in which you and someone else talk about ice-cream rain.

_____ : _____

_____ : _____

_____ : _____

_____ : _____

_____ : _____

_____ : _____

What's the Game?

There are many kinds of games or sports. List some games you like to play or watch. What if people don't know about a sport? You can tell them.

Pick a sport. Then follow these steps:

1. Start with this line: **I am going to tell you about a sport I like.**

2. Say what you need to play.

3. Say if it is a team or individual sport.

4. Tell what the players do or how they score.

5. End your speech with: **So what is the name of my sport? It is _____!**

I am going to tell you about a sport I like.

_____

_____

_____

_____

_____

So what is the name of my sport?   It is _____!

Practice reading your speech to yourself. Then read your speech to the class or a friend.

You are a sports announcer. Your voice is heard over the loudspeakers and the radio. Write down what you might say. Pick a sport you are watching. Then get ready to write.

Follow these steps:

1. Start with this line: **Good afternoon, _____ fans!**
   (sport name)

2. Say a player's name and where he or she is.

3. Describe what the player does on the field or court.

4. Write a line telling if the team or person scores, wins, or loses.

5. End your announcement with: **This is _____ signing off.**
   (your name)

Good afternoon, _____ fans!
                            (sport name)

_____

_____

_____

This is _____ signing off.
                    (your name)

Practice reading your announcement to yourself. When you read, think about how announcers make their voices sound excited or upset. Be ready to read your announcement to the class or a friend.

Three, Two, One

Writers use short sentences. Writers use long sentences. Writers use short and long sentences so that the writing is not all the same. The short and long sentences help to keep the reader from getting bored.

Think of three things you like to eat or do. Write one sentence about each thing. Then turn the three sentences into two sentences. Next, turn the two sentences into one sentence.

Example

3– I like carrots. I like peas. I like tomatoes.

2– I like carrots and peas. I like tomatoes, too.

1– I like carrots, peas, and tomatoes.

3–   I like _____.   I like _____.

I like _____.

2–   I like _____.

I like _____.

1–   I like _____

_____.

Short and Long

Changing the sentence length helps keep the reader from getting bored. Practice writing short and long sentences.

Imagine that you are an animal. Think of three things the animal would like to eat or do. Write one sentence about each thing. Then turn the three sentences into two sentences. Next, turn the two sentences into one sentence.

Example

Animal: The Horse

3–　I like to jump.　I like to run.　I like to eat hay.

2–　I like to jump and run.　I like to eat hay, too.

1–　I like to jump, run, and eat hay.

Animal: _____

3–　I like _____. I like _____.

　　I like _____.

2–　I like _____.

　　I like _____.

1–　I like _____.

　　_____.

To the Top!

Mt. Everest is the highest mountain in the world. Hillary and Norgay were the first to climb to the top. They reached the top on May 29, 1953.

Read the sentences. Then write the two sentences as one sentence. Use the word **and**.

> ### Example
> 1. It is very cold on Mt. Everest.
> 2. It is very dangerous on Mt. Everest.
>
> It is very cold and dangerous on Mt. Everest.

1. Hillary climbed Mt. Everest.
2. Norgay climbed Mt. Everest.

_____

1. The air was thin.
2. The air was hard to breathe.

_____

1. They used ropes.
2. They used bottled oxygen.

_____

The Climber

Imagine you are climbing Mt. Everest. What are some things you might see, wear, and feel? Write information in short sentences, then combine the sentences. Use the word **and**.

Example

1. I see white snow.

2. I see steep rocks.

I see white snow and steep rocks.

Write two sentences about what you might wear on Mt. Everest. Then, combine the sentences. Use the word **and**.

1. I am wearing _____.

2. I am wearing _____.

I am wearing _____.

Write two sentences about how you might feel on Mt. Everest. Then, combine the sentences. Use the word **and**.

1. I feel _____.

2. I feel _____.

I feel _____.

First, Second, Third

You are going to brush your teeth. How do you do it? You do it in steps. Write **first**, **second**, and **third** by the steps to show what order they go in.

_____ , rinse your mouth.
(First, Second, Third)

_____ , brush your teeth all over.
(First, Second, Third)

_____ , put toothpaste on brush.
(First, Second, Third)

When you write, you want to put the how-to steps in the right order. This helps the reader understand.

You are going to teach someone how to make a bowl of cereal. Think of three steps. What will you do first? What will you do last?

Complete the sentences.

First, _____

_____.

Second, _____

_____.

Third, _____

_____.

Shoes First

Imagine that a creature from outer space comes to visit. The visitor has never seen "Earth" clothes. You tell the creature to get dressed, so the creature picks up your shoes and says, "I will put these on first."

◆◆◆◆◆◆◆◆◆◆◆◆◆◆◆◆◆◆◆◆

Help the space creature get dressed by writing out how-to steps. Think about what must be done first.

First, _____

_____.

Second, _____

_____.

Third, _____

_____.

Fourth, _____

_____.

Fifth, _____

_____.

Sometimes we need to send out invitations. In the invitation, we need to include the date and time, and where the event is taking place. Often we need to include special instructions.

> ## Example
>
> To: Sam H.
> What: A birthday party for Zoey
> Date: May 5, 2012
> Time: 4:00 PM to 6:00 PM
> Place: 25 Chicken Lane
> Be Ready: Wear old clothes because we will dig for treasure!

Make an invitation to a party you would like to have one day. Then draw a picture for your invitation on the back of this page.

Party Invitation!

To: _____

What: _____

Date: _____

Time: _____

Place: _____

Be Ready: _____

Surprise Party!

Imagine that you are planning a surprise party for someone. Write out an invitation to the party.

Think ahead:

◆ Should people get there early or late?

◆ Should people talk about it before?

Party Invitation!

To: _____

What: _____

Date: _____

Time: _____

Place: _____

Be Ready: _____

_____

Thank-You Note

It is good manners to write thank-you notes. You can write thank-you notes for gifts or visits.

Example

March 3

Dear Aunt Patty,

Thank you for taking me on a picnic. I liked feeding the birds at the park.

Sincerely,
Jerome

Practice writing a thank-you note. In your note, you should say something about the gift or visit.

_____
(date)

Dear _____,

_____

_____

_____

_____,
(Your friend, Sincerely, Love)

_____
(name)

Imagine that you get a box in the mail. It is from your Uncle Juan. You open it up, and what do you find? You find a jellyfish!

No matter how you feel, you need to send a thank-you note.

Decide what you will say about the jellyfish. Were you surprised? What might you do with it? Where might you keep it? What might you name it?

_____
(date)

Dear Uncle Juan,

_____

_____

_____

_____

Your _____,
(nephew/niece)

_____
(name)

Now draw a picture of a jellyfish on the back of this page.

Big and Small

The ostrich is the biggest bird. The bee hummingbird is the smallest bird.

Writers can pick how they give information.

They can say:

The ostrich is **bigger than** the bee hummingbird.

The bee hummingbird is **smaller than** the ostrich.

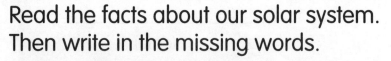

Read the facts about our solar system.
Then write in the missing words.

Jupiter is the biggest planet. Mercury is the smallest planet.

Jupiter is _____ the planet Mercury.

Mercury is _____ the planet Jupiter.

Now use the facts below to write out your own two sentences with the words **bigger than** and **smaller than**.

The blue whale is the biggest whale. The dwarf sperm whale is the smallest whale.

_____

_____

_____

_____

Pete and Penny

Look at Pete. Look at Penny. Compare Pete to Penny.
Then compare Penny to Pete.

> ### Example
> 1. Pete is bigger than Penny.
> 2. Penny is smaller than Pete.

Use the words **longer, shorter, bigger,** and **smaller** when you compare Pete to Penny.

Compare their legs.

1. **Pete has** _____ .

2. **Penny has** _____ .

Compare their paws.

1. **Pete has** _____ .

2. **Penny has** _____ .

Write two sentences. In them, compare yourself to Pete or Penny.

_____

_____

_____

What if you went to the beach?

Answer the questions. Put a check in each box when you have answered the question. You can write a separate sentence for each answer, or you can put two answers in one sentence.

☐ What would I bring or wear?

☐ What would I see?   ☐ What would I do?

☐ What would I hear?   ☐ What would I feel?

At the beach, I would _____

_____

_____

_____

_____

_____

_____

_____

Where You Have Never Gone

Pick a place you have never gone:

> **under the water**   rainforest   Antarctica   desert   volcano

Now imagine you are at this place. Do not say where you are, but answer the questions. Put a check in each box when you have answered the question.

- ☐ What would I bring and/or wear?
- ☐ What would I see?
- ☐ What would I hear?
- ☐ What would I do?
- ☐ What would I feel?

_____

_____

_____

_____

_____

When it is your turn, read your answers out loud to the class. Then ask, **"Where am I?"**

Did your answers help people to tell which place you were imagining?

The Oregon Trail

In 1846, a man went from Iowa to Oregon. His name was Henderson Luelling. He went on the Oregon Trail. He brought two extra wagons. What was in the wagons? The wagons were filled with dirt and fruit trees!

◆◆◆◆◆◆◆◆◆◆◆◆◆◆◆◆◆◆

People kept journals or diaries while traveling. The diaries help us learn about life on the Oregon Trail.

Write a journal entry for Mr. Luelling.

In your journal entry, include:

♦ what it is like to travel with wagons full of fruit tees
♦ one thing you have to do to keep the trees alive
♦ one thing you hope to do with the trees

Journal for Henderson Luelling

Date: _____

Place: _____

_____

_____

_____

_____

A New Place

Long ago, many people went on the Oregon Trail. They could not fly or drive. They had to walk. They walked fifteen miles a day for six months. Often, they walked barefoot. People had to be careful about what they brought. They did not have much space. The wagons could not be too heavy.

◆◆◆◆◆◆◆◆◆◆◆◆◆◆◆◆◆◆◆

Imagine that you are moving to a new place. Write a journal entry. Use your imagination.

In your journal entry, include:

◆ where you started and where you hope to go

◆ how you are getting there

◆ one thing you might bring and why

Journal for _____

Date: _____

_____

_____

_____

_____

_____

Have you ever lost something? When people lose things, they sometimes put up signs. The signs say what they have lost. The signs must have details so people know exactly what was lost.

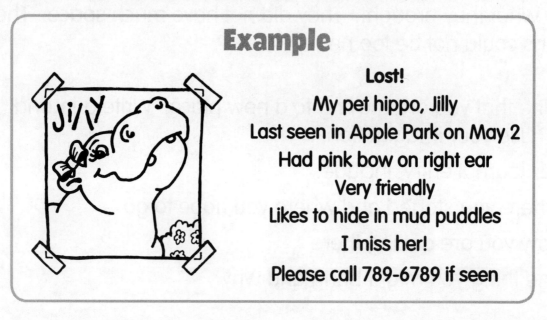

Example

Lost!
My pet hippo, Jilly
Last seen in Apple Park on May 2
Had pink bow on right ear
Very friendly
Likes to hide in mud puddles
I miss her!
Please call 789-6789 if seen

Think of something you have lost. You can think of a real thing or a made-up thing. Then make a sign. Use lots of details.

Lost!

_____

_____

_____

_____

_____

Voice

Lion at the Movies

One city had a law. The law was that no one could take a lion to the movies. Some people call this law silly.

Write why you think the law was made.

Write if you think the law is silly or not and why.

Write if you think the law is needed or not and why.

_____

_____

_____

_____

_____

_____

_____

Crocodile at the Pool

You go to a swimming pool. The swimming pool is for all the children. You are about to jump in. Then you see a crocodile in the water! The child next to you says, "Oh, don't mind that crocodile. It's my pet."

◆◆◆◆◆◆◆◆◆◆◆◆◆◆◆◆◆◆

What do you think? Is it okay for the crocodile to be in the pool? Tell why or why not.

_____

_____

_____

_____

_____

_____

_____

_____

The Best Pet

Many people have pets. The most popular pets are cats and dogs. There are more pet cats than pet dogs.

Which one is the best pet, a cat or a dog? There is no right answer. There is no wrong answer. It is up to you.

Decide what the best pet is. Then think of some reasons why it is the best. Write down what your best pet pick is and why.

Start your first sentence with one of these phrases:

> I think   I believe   I feel

_____

_____

_____

_____

_____

_____

The Happy Seal

You are walking home from school. When you get to your door, you find a happy seal on the doorstep. The happy seal says, "I want to be your pet."

Is a seal a good pet for you? Tell why or why not.

When you answer, think about:

- ◆ where you live
- ◆ what seals eat

_____

_____

_____

_____

_____

_____

_____

Yellowstone

You want to go to Yellowstone Park. Before you go, you want information. What is there to see? What can you do?

Write a letter asking for information. Write a formal letter.

For this type of letter, you include your address and the address where you are sending the letter. You include the date. You end it with the word, "**Sincerely.**"

Your school address:

_____

_____

_____

(date)

Yellowstone National Park

P.O Box 168

Yellowstone National Park, WY

82190-0168

Dear Yellowstone Ranger:

_____

_____

_____

Sincerely,

_____

(first and last name)

Old Faithful

Imagine that you went to Yellowstone. You saw the geyser Old Faithful. Write a letter to a friend about your trip and what you saw.

Your letter to your friend does not have to be formal. You can include words and phrases you like to use. It can be silly or serious.

Danger!

Watch for boiling water!

Old Faithful shoots water over 100 feet high!

Possible adjectives: *amazing, great, wonderful, thrilling, boring*

Possible endings: *Love, Your friend, Your pal, Goodbye for now*

_____
(date)

Dear _____ ,

_____

_____

_____

_____ ,

_____

Skateboarder Hawk

Tony Hawk is a skateboarder. Tony does dangerous flips. He has turned around in the air. He has won many titles. He has crashed many times. He runs skateboarding camps. He makes up games.

What interests you most about Tony? If you could ask him some questions, what would they be?

Write a dialogue. In it, interview Tony. First, greet Tony in your own, natural way. Then ask questions that interest you. Make up your own answers for Tony.

_____ : _____
  (your name)

Tony : _____

_____ : _____

Tony : _____

_____ : _____

Tony : _____

Learning Something New

Tony Hawk got on a skateboard. It was his brother's old skateboard. It was Tony's first time. Tony went down the driveway. He got to the end of the driveway. He did not know what to do. He asked his brother, "How do I turn?"

◆◆◆◆◆◆◆◆◆◆◆◆◆◆◆◆◆◆◆

Think about something you did for the first time. It could be swimming, riding a bike, jumping rope, or something else. How did you learn? What questions did you ask? How did you feel?

Write an imaginary dialogue. In it, tell Tony what you learned. Tell Tony what you did and how you felt before, during, or after you learned it.

You can have Tony ask questions, or you can have him say things like, "Oh, no!" "Wow!" "You're kidding!" "That is amazing!"

_____ : _____
  (your name)

Tony : _____

_____ : _____

Tony : _____

_____ : _____

Tony : _____

_____ : _____

Yellow Walls

Voice

In some countries, like Finland, it is dark all day in the winter. Some people get sad in the dark. What do people do? They paint their walls yellow. The bright color helps them not be so sad.

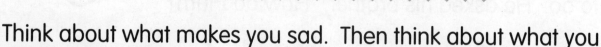

Think about what makes you sad. Then think about what you might do to feel better. Think about what makes you happy.

Now write a few sentences describing something that makes you sad. Then tell what you can do to feel better.

_____

_____

_____

_____

_____

_____

_____

_____

Painted Rooms

You wake up and see that all the walls in your home have been painted. They all have bright pink and green stripes!

Write a few sentences and tell what you think.

- ◆ Would you keep the striped walls or repaint them?
- ◆ Would you paint over every wall or in just some of the rooms?
- ◆ What colors would you choose for what rooms and why?

_____

_____

_____

_____

_____

_____

_____

_____

When What?

You feel different ways at different times. Think of times when you feel happy, sad, excited, scared, and interested. Each person has different feelings, so everything you feel is right.

I am happy when _____

_____.

I am sad when _____

_____.

I am excited when _____

_____.

I am scared when _____

_____.

I am interested when _____

_____.

On the back of this paper, draw at least two faces that match two of the feelings in the list. Write what feeling each face is showing under the face.

The Dog and the Bone

A dog had a bone. The bone was in his mouth. The dog went across a bridge. That dog looked down at the water. He saw another dog in the water. That dog had a bone, too. "That bone looks better than my bone. I want that bone!" said the dog on the bridge. He opened his mouth to bark at the other dog and get the bone. What happened? The dog on the bridge had been staring at his own reflection! When the dog opened his mouth to bark, his bone fell into the water. Now the dog had nothing.

◆◆◆◆◆◆◆◆◆◆◆◆◆◆◆◆◆◆

Write how you think the dog felt during different parts of the story and why.

In the beginning of the story, the dog felt _____

_____.

When the dog saw the other bone, he felt _____

_____.

At the end of the story, the dog felt _____

_____.

Night Sounds

Voice

88

Have you ever been outside at night? Perhaps you were around a campfire, or in your backyard. Perhaps you were taking a walk with your family.

Think of a time when you were outside at night.

Where were you and what were you doing?

_____

_____

_____

What did you see and hear?

_____

_____

Write about how you felt.

_____

_____

The Owl

Owls sleep during the day. Owls hunt at night.

Imagine that you are an owl. Write a few sentences about what it is like to be out at night.

Where are you? What do you see? Do you see something to catch? What do you do when you see it?

When you write, use the word I. That is because in the story, you are the owl.

_____

_____

_____

_____

_____

_____

_____

Seasons

There are four seasons: winter, spring, summer, and fall. People like different things about different seasons.

Look at the two poems. What person likes winter better?

Winter	Winter
Dark days	Snow like white flowers days
Cold and freezing days	Sledding down hills days
Stay indoor days	Building forts with friends days
Bare trees days	Warm jackets to wear days
Want to stay in bed days	Happy to drink hot chocolate days
Winter	Winter

Write about summer. Do you like it or not? Write a poem like the examples above. In your poem, describe some of the things you can see, do, or feel.

Summer

_____

_____

_____

_____

Summer

The Opposite

Sometimes it is fun to write about the opposite of what you think.

Write an opposite poem. Think about spring. Do you love it, or are there things you don't like about spring?

Think before you write! What are some things you like and things you don't like about spring?

Things I Like	Things I Don't Like
_____	_____
_____	_____
_____	_____
_____	_____

Now write the opposite of what you think. This is practice for writing from a different viewpoint.

Spring

_____

_____

_____

_____

Spring

A Favorite Spot

You must have a place you like to be. Is it a park? It is a room? Is it under a special tree? Is it a grandparent's house?

Think about a place that is a favorite. Write a few sentences about your favorite spot.

Tell where it is.

_____

_____

Describe what it looks like.

_____

_____

Tell why this place is special to you.

_____

_____

_____

On the back of this paper, draw a picture of your favorite place.

Pig's Place

How do you stay cool? You sweat. Pigs cannot sweat like you can. They have to stay cool another way. When it gets hot, they get in cool mud. The mud keeps them cool.

Imagine that it is a hot day, and you need to cool down.

Tell where you would go to cool down. _____

_____

_____

Describe what it looks like. _____

_____

_____

Would it be the same place a pig would go? Why or why not?

_____

_____

_____

Name Writing

How do people get ready to teach? Sometimes they write out lessons. Then they say the lessons out loud.

Write out a lesson. In it, teach someone how to write your first name.

Hello. This morning I am going to teach you how to

write my name. My name is _____ .

My name has _____ letters.

It has _____ vowels.

First, you write a capital letter _____.

Next, _____

_____

_____ .

Put it all together and it spells _____.

Now let's write my name in the air! Ready?

State Writing

Voice

A visitor comes to your school. The visitor is from a different state. The visitor asks you how to spell the name of your state. Write out what you will say to the visitor.

Will you teach one, two, or three letters at a time?

Complete the instructions:

Hello. This morning I am going to teach you how to write our state name. Our state name is

_____.

It has _____ letters.

It has _____ vowels.

First, you write a capital letter _____.

Next, _____

_____

_____.

Put it all together and it spells

_____.

Abe's Trick

Long ago, Abe Lincoln was president. Before he was president, he played a trick. He had a small boy walk in mud. Then, he held the boy upside down. The small boy left muddy footprints on the ceiling!

◆◆◆◆◆◆◆◆◆◆◆◆◆◆◆◆◆◆

Write a journal entry for Abe. In your journal entry, talk about the trick. Use the word **I** since you are writing as if you were Abe.

Abe Lincoln's Journal

June 21, 1817

Today _____

_____

_____

_____

_____

_____

_____

King Midas

Voice

King Midas loved gold. He loved gold more than anything. King Midas wished that everything he touched would turn to gold. King Midas got his wish. At first he was happy. He turned things to gold. Then he found he could not eat. Then he turned his daughter to gold. King Midas took his wish back.

◆◆◆◆◆◆◆◆◆◆◆◆◆◆◆◆◆◆

Write a journal entry for King Midas. In your journal entry, write about your wish. Say if it was a good or bad wish. Use the word **I** since you are writing as if you were King Midas. Say if you would make the wish again.

King Midas's Journal

April 4, 760

_____

_____

_____

_____

A Hero

A hero is someone you look up to. You admire a hero. Your hero may be honest, strong, or kind. Your hero may be famous or not famous. Everyone has different heroes.

Write a few sentences about one of your heroes. When you write, be sure to:

☐ tell who the person is

☐ tell what he or she does or how you know this person

☐ tell what you admire about this person

Put a check in each box after you have done each thing.

My hero is _____

_____

_____

_____

_____

_____

_____

_____

Superpower!

Some heroes have superpowers. The superheroes can fly or see things far away. If you could have a superpower, what would it be? Would it be super eyes, ears, speed, or strength? Would it be knowing how to fly or being invisible? You pick!

Once you have picked your superpower, write:

☐ what the superpower is

☐ what you can or would do with your superpower

☐ why you chose this superpower

Put a check in each box after you have done each thing.

If I could choose a superpower, I would pick _____

_____

_____

_____

_____

_____

_____

Splat!

Bang!   Splat!   Crash!   Pow!

All of these words make you pay attention. They make you think of a loud sound. They make you think of action.

Write a sentence after each word that explains the sound. The sentences can be about real or made-up events or things.

> **Example**
> Splat! The elephant stepped on the banana!

Pow! _____

_____

Bang! _____

_____

Crash! _____

_____

Organization

Story Start

Writers use special words to let readers know when something starts. They use different words at the end of a story. These words help the reader.

What is most likely the beginning of a story?

1. a. Once upon a time   b. At last

2. a. In the end   b. When my dad was little

3. a. Yesterday   b. Finally

Think of a way to start a story about yourself. Write one or two lines of the story, starting from the beginning. You do not have to write the end. What words will you choose to start?

_____

_____

_____

Can you think of another way to start the same story? Write another beginning here.

_____

_____

_____

The Tortoise and the Rabbit

The tortoise won.
The rabbit lost.
The rabbit took a nap.
The rabbit ran faster.
The rabbit fell asleep.
Once upon a time, there was a race.
The tortoise never stopped.

◆◆◆◆◆◆◆◆◆◆◆◆◆◆◆◆◆◆◆◆◆

Was it hard to understand the story? The story did not start at the beginning. It was all mixed up.

Rewrite the story. Put what happened in the right order.

The Tortoise and the Rabbit

_____

_____

_____

_____

_____

_____

103

Talking on the Phone

When you answer the phone, what do you say?

    A. Goodbye   **B. Hello**

Write down a phone conversation you might have. The phone conversation should be between you and another person you know.

Make sure your conversation has a proper beginning and ending. In the conversation, ask the person to go somewhere or do something with you.

Name of person talking	**What the person says**
_____ :	_____
_____ :	_____
_____ :	_____
_____ :	_____
_____ :	_____
_____ :	_____
_____ :	_____
_____ :	_____

Which riddle is told in the right order?

    A. **What kind of stones do you never find in the ocean? Dry ones!**

    B. **Dry ones! What kind of stones do you never find in the ocean?**

Write down a conversation. In it, tell someone a riddle. Make sure you tell the riddle in the right order! You may use a riddle from this page, or you may use your own.

Remember to write down what you think the person will say after you tell him or her the riddle. Will you have the person answer the riddle correctly or say, "I don't know" or "What?"

_____ : _____

  (your name)

_____ : _____

_____ : _____

_____ : _____

What did one wall say to the other wall?
Meet you at the corner!

    What time is it if you see an elephant in a car?
    Time to get a new car!

        What do lazy dogs do?
        Chase parked cars!

The First Voyage of Columbus

Where did Columbus sail on his first voyage? He sailed from Spain. He went to islands in what was known as the "New World."

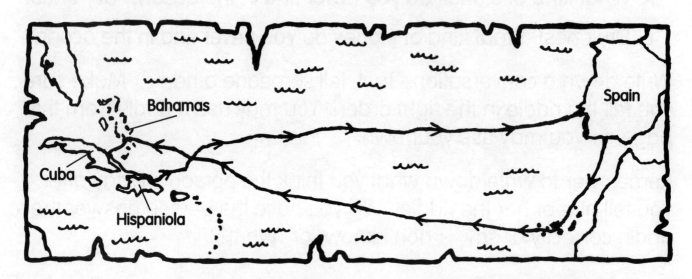

Tell about Columbus's trip with complete sentences. Keep the order straight! You can start your sentences any way you like.

> ## Ways to start your sentences:
>
> First   Second   Third   Next   Then   Finally

First, Columbus sailed from Spain to the Bahamas.

_____

_____

_____

_____

Treasure Hunt

You are on a treasure hunt. You must follow the map. You must go in the correct order to find the clues.

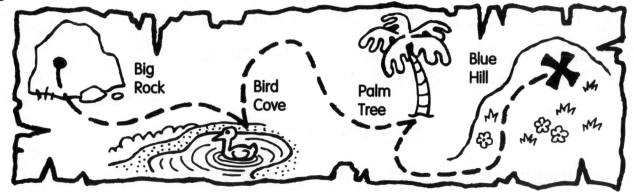

Write down where you go to find the treasure using complete sentences. You can start your sentences any way you like.

First or To start?	Second or Next?	At last or Finally?

How to Find the Treasure

_____

_____

_____

_____

_____

_____

_____

The Coat Hanger

One day in 1903, Albert Parkhouse went to work. When he got there, all the hooks had coats on them. There was no place to hang his coat. Albert took a piece of wire. He bent it.

He made a coat hanger! Today lots of people hang their coats on hangers.

Many stories have problems. The first part of the story says what the problem is. The last part of the story says how the problem is solved.

Answer these questions about the story.

Who had the problem? _____

When was there a problem? _____

Where was the problem? _____

What was the problem? _____

_____

How was the problem solved? _____

_____

_____

Lost and Found

Imagine that there is a problem. The problem is that something is lost. You decide if the lost something is a person, a thing, or an animal.

Make up some details about the problem:

Who or what is lost? _____

When was it lost? _____

Where was it lost? _____

_____

Why was it lost? _____

_____

_____

How was it found? _____

_____

_____

What Pup?

You are going to give a speech. The speech is to tell people about a pup. What pup? You must say what kind of pup you are talking about so no one gets confused.

Chose a pup. Then write what you will say about the pup. Use some of the facts in the chart.

Dog Pup	Bat Pup
Drinks milk	Drinks milk
Walks on ground	Hangs upside down
More than one born at a time	Only one born at a time
Mom keeps pups away from other dogs	May live with many other bats

I am going to talk about a pup that is a baby _____ .

This kind of pup _____

_____

_____

_____

_____

Who Is Knocking?

A baby mole is called a pup. A baby armadillo is called a pup. Baby sharks, guinea pigs, and seals are called pups, too.

Imagine that you hear a knock on the door. A pup is knocking at the door. Write down what happens next. Make sure you choose what type of pup it is!

One day, I heard a knock at the door. _____

_____

_____

_____

_____

_____

_____

_____

_____

Roof Ride

News reports tell **who, what, where, when,** and **why**. Use the facts below to write a news report. Think of a short, interesting headline (title) for your story.

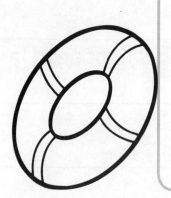

Who: Mr. Shinkawa

What: Rescue from his house roof

Where: 9 miles off coast of Japan

When: March 13, 2011

Why: Roof swept to sea by tsunami

Headline: _____

_____

_____

_____

_____

_____

_____

Two Days at Sea

A tsunami hit Japan on March 11, 2011. The big wave swept Mr. Shinkawa and his roof out to sea. Mr. Shinkawa floated on his roof for two days. Then he was saved.

Imagine you are Mr. Shinkawa. Write about what happened to you. How did you feel at first and at the end? Did you think you were going to be saved?

_____

_____

_____

_____

_____

_____

_____

The Sun

In some poems, people compare things. A writer will write about a real thing. Then, he or she will compare the thing to something else. This helps the reader know how the writer feels about the thing.

Two Examples

The sun	It is like a blanket
Is like a blanket	That covers us and
That covers us and	Keeps us warm.
Keeps us warm.	It is the sun.

Pick a real thing. It may be a tree, a plane, a book, happiness, or anything else you want! Then say what it is like. You can say what the thing is at the beginning or end of the poem.

_____

_____

_____

_____

_____

Think of how animals move. Animals can move in all kinds of ways. A horse may run, walk, gallop, trot, or jump.

Write a poem. In it, write:

◆ that you are like an animal

◆ how you moved like the animal and went some place

◆ what you did at the place

> **Example**
>
> Like a rabbit
> I hopped to the moon
> And ate cheese with a spoon.

_____

_____

_____

_____

_____

Where in the School?

Stories are set in all kinds of places. What if a story was set at your school?

Describe one room inside your school. It could be your classroom, the library, or any other place you want.

When you write, think about:

◆ The floors—the color, carpet or tile

◆ The walls—the color, what is on them

◆ The windows—the size, how many, where

◆ What is in the room—desks, sinks, chairs, animals

Don't say what room you are talking about until the end!

There is a room in my school that has _____

_____

_____

_____

_____

What room is this? It is _____.

Read the beginning out loud. Did you give enough details that people could tell what room it was?

The Secret Tunnel

Imagine you are writing a story about a secret tunnel. You have to plan the tunnel.

Think of answers to these questions. Then write about the tunnel.

◆ Where does it start and end?

◆ How do you hide its entrance and get in?

◆ How can you move when you are inside?

◆ Will you need a light?

_____

_____

_____

_____

_____

_____

_____

_____

Eating an Orange

What if you had never seen an orange? Would you know how to eat it? Or would you think it was like an apple and try to bite it, skin and all?

Write down how to eat an orange.

In your how-to, you might want to use these words:

peel   section

In your last step or steps, write, **"Eat plain or with** _____ **,"** and then list some foods you can put oranges in.

How to Eat an Orange

1. _____

2. _____

3. _____

4. _____

5. _____

_____

_____

The Wrong Banana

Zippa says, "You gave me the wrong banana. The banana you are eating is soft. It is very pale. The banana you gave me is bright yellow. I took a bite, but it tasted bad. It was so hard I could not bite into it."

◆◆◆◆◆◆◆◆◆◆◆◆◆◆◆◆◆◆

Zippa needs a lesson in how to eat a banana. Write a how-to for Zippa.

In your last step or steps, write, **"Eat plain or with** _____**,"** and then list some foods you can make or eat with bananas.

How to Eat a Banana

1. _____

2. _____

3. _____

4. _____

5. _____

_____

_____

Where's the Lemonade?

Read this sign:

Lemonade Sale!

The Best Lemonade!

The Best Price!

People make signs all the time. The signs tell what, where, and when. Read the sign again. Circle the two things it does not tell.

what   when   where

Make a sign that gives people all the information they need for a lemonade sale. Make sure you mention:

What—what is for sale

When—day and time

Where—location

You can include the price if you want. You can also include drawings or words that make people want to buy the lemonade.

_____

_____

_____

_____

Gobble It Down!

You have invented a new food. You are having a sale of your new food. You will give away free samples at your sale.

Make up a name for your new food. Then make a sign for your sale. Your sign should tell people **what, when,** and **where.**

Add pictures, words, and phrases to your sign that explain your food or make people want to gobble it down.

Ben and the Turkey

Ben Franklin lived long ago. He helped the United States be a new country. The new country had a new flag. Now it needed a bird. The bird would stand for the country. The bird would be the national bird. What bird did Ben want? Ben wanted the turkey.

◆◆◆◆◆◆◆◆◆◆◆◆◆◆◆◆◆◆◆

You have read the beginning of the story. You have read the middle of the story. Now it is your turn to write the end of the story.

When you write, tell that Ben's bird was not chosen. Tell what bird is the national bird today.

_____

_____

_____

_____

_____

_____

_____

Ben and the Fire

One day, Ben saw a fire. The fire was small, but no one was there to help put it out. The fire got bigger. It got bigger and bigger. Soon, the house burned down. Ben said, "This is not good. We have to find a way to stop fires when they are small."

◆◆◆◆◆◆◆◆◆◆◆◆◆◆◆◆◆◆◆◆

You have read the beginning of the story. You have read the middle of the story. Now it is your turn to write the end of the story. Imagine you are Ben. Think about what Ben will say and do.

Use this information when you write the end of the story: *Ben set up the first volunteer fire department.*

"I know what we can do," said Ben. _____

_____

_____

_____

_____

_____

_____

The School Day

Think about how your school day starts. Think about what you do in the middle of your school day. Think about what you do at the end.

Write down things you do at different times of the day.

At the beginning of the school day, _____

_____

_____

_____.

In the middle of the school day, _____

_____

_____

_____.

At the end of the school day, _____

_____

_____

_____.

The Cat's Work

Some people say that a cat sleeps all day. Do you think this is true?

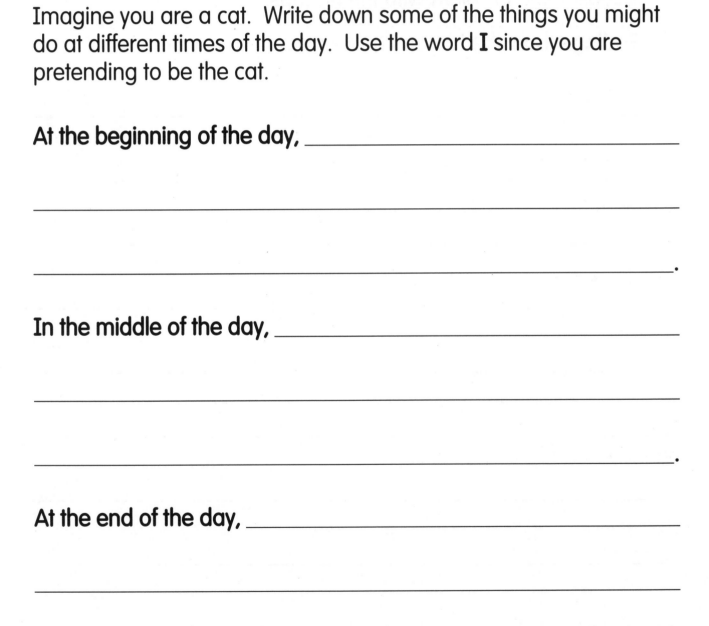

Imagine you are a cat. Write down some of the things you might do at different times of the day. Use the word **I** since you are pretending to be the cat.

At the beginning of the day, _____

_____

_____.

In the middle of the day, _____

_____

_____.

At the end of the day, _____

_____

_____.

The Hiccups

Write a story with a beginning, middle, and end. You can write about yourself, another real person, or someone you make up. The person in the story had the hiccups. Tell how the hiccups were made to go away.

Beginning—who and where

Middle—the problem with the hiccups

Ending—how the hiccups go away

_____

_____

_____

_____

_____

_____

_____

_____

_____

Conventions

Big City/Small City

There are big cities. There are small cities. Big or small, all city names start with capital letters. People's first and last names start with capital letters, too.

Which two things should start with capital letters?

   a. name of a city   **b. name of a fruit**   **c. your last name**

Correct the sentences by making sure all the city and people names start with capital letters.

> taylor and annie live in helena.
>
> max and cody live in san francisco.

Now show what you know! Write a test sentence. In your test sentence, have one or two city or people names that **are not** capitalized. Then, write the sentence correctly on the back of this page.

_____

_____

_____

Show your test sentence to your classmates. Can they spot the names that need capital letters?

When you write, you make up people to write about. You get to make up where people live, too. Even when the names of people and places are made up, they need to start with capital letters.

Correct the sentences by making sure all the people and place names start with capital letters.

mollie moose lives in madison.

mike mouse lives in hartford.

ellen elephant lives in los angeles.

Now show what you know! Write a test sentence about someone you made up. In your test sentence, have one or two names or places that **are not** capitalized. Then write the sentence correctly on the back of this page.

_____

_____

_____

Be ready to show your test sentence to your classmates. Can they spot the words that need capital letters?

The Escape Man

The first word of every sentence is always capitalized. This helps you know when a sentence is starting.

What word is always capitalized in a sentence?

   a. last   b. middle   c. first

Correct the following sentences by making sure that the first word in each sentence starts with a capital letter.

> houdini liked to escape. he could escape from handcuffs. he could escape from ropes. he could escape from chains. why was he so good at escaping? he could hide tools. he could untie knots with his fingers and his toes!

Write a sentence or two about Houdini. Tell where or how you think he hid his tools. When you are done, check to make sure the first word in each sentence starts with a capital letter.

_____

_____

_____

The Egg

Every sentence starts with a capital letter. This means the **first** word is always capitalized.

What part of the sentence always has a capital letter?

   a. **the beginning**   b. **the end**

Correct the following sentences by making sure that the first word in each sentence starts with a capital letter.

> a king said, "Show me something new. show me something no king has seen." no one could show the king something new. at last a small boy came. the small boy showed the king an egg. everyone laughed at the small boy. then the egg started to hatch.

Now think about what might happen if the egg hatches. Will the king see something new?

Write a sentence or two to finish the story. When you are done, check to make sure the first word of each sentence starts with a capital letter.

_____

_____

_____

The Biggest Animal

Read the two sentences. Which sentence is a question?

    a. **What is the biggest land animal?**

    b. **The biggest land animal is an elephant.**

What goes at the end of a question?

    a. .   b. ?

Correct the following sentences by putting in periods (.) or question marks (**?**).

> Something landed on an elephant's skin   The elephant could feel what landed on its skin   What landed on the elephant's skin   Was it big or small   It was small   It was a fly!

Write two sentences about an elephant. One sentence should be a question. When you are done, check to make sure the right marks are at the ends of your sentences.

_____

_____

_____

_____

The Fastest Animal

Read the two sentences. Which sentence is a question?

a. **The cheetah is the fastest land animal.**

b. **What animal is the fastest land animal?**

What goes at the end of a question?

a. **.**   b. **?**

Correct the following sentences by putting in periods (.) or question marks (**?**).

My name is Felix   What am I   I am a cheetah
Can I run faster than a horse   Yes, I can   Can I
run faster than a car   I can run 70 miles per hour!

Write two sentences about Felix. One sentence should be a question. When you are done, check to make sure the right marks are at the ends of your sentences.

_____

_____

_____

_____

What has eight arms? A squid has eight arms.
What did the squid eat? The squid ate a small fish. It
ate a crab. It ate eight shrimp.

Go back to the sentences above.
Circle these words:

eight (3 times)   **ate** (3 times)

Do the words **eight** and **ate** sound
the same?

a. no   b. yes

Are the words **eight** and **ate** spelled
the same?

a. no   b. yes

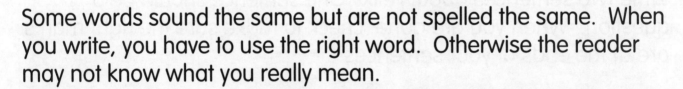

Some words sound the same but are not spelled the same. When
you write, you have to use the right word. Otherwise the reader
may not know what you really mean.

Write a sentence or two with the words **eight** and **ate**. Make sure
the spelling matches the meaning!

_____

_____

_____

See the Sea

Do you see the sea?
Yes, I see the sea.

Write the two words that sound the same in the sentences above.

1. _____   2. _____

Do the sentences below make sense? _____

Do you sea the see?
Yes, I sea the see.

Find and correct the 8 misspelled words below.

> Tim went to the see. What did he sea at the see?
> Tim saw ate fish. Tim eight one of the fish. What
> did he sea at the see? Tim saw ate boats. Tim did
> not eat one of the boats!

Write a sentence with this word pair: **one/won**. When you are
done, check that your spelling matches the meaning you wanted.

_____

_____

How Do You Hear?

The words **hear** and **here** sound the same. They do not mean the same thing.

What do you use to hear?   **a. ear**   **b. eye**

Circle the word **ear** in **hear**.   h e a r

Correct the 5 misspelled words in the story.

> How do we here? We here with our ears. Our ears
>
> are hear on our heads. A cricket is hear. How does
>
> a cricket here? A cricket uses its legs.

Now it is your turn to be the teacher. Write a sentence or two. In them, misspell some words from the list below. Put the number of misspelled words in the box at the bottom of the page.

> son   sun   ant   aunt   sail   sale

_____

_____

Number of misspelled words:

Show your sentences to a friend. Could your friend find all the misspelled words?

The Woodchuck

Would the woodchuck chop wood? This is what the woodchuck wrote:

> I wood.
>
> I wood chop would.
>
> I wood chop would if I could chop would.

Help the woodchuck with his spelling. Go back and correct the six words the woodchuck misspelled.

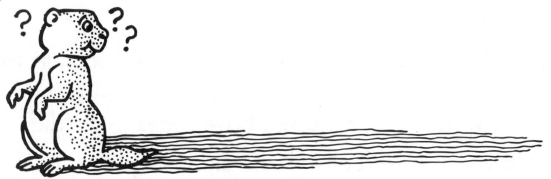

A woodchuck is also known as a groundhog.

Write a sentence or two about what a make-believe groundhog would do if it saw its shadow on February 2.

_____

_____

_____

_____

Exciting Sport

Something is wrong with these sentences:

My name is Pele!!!! I play soccer!!!!!

What is wrong with all the exclamation points (!!!!!!!!!)?

a. not enough   b. too many

Exclamation points go at the ends of some sentences. They are used to show excitement. You don't need them for every sentence. You only use one at a time.

Correct the sentences below by putting a mark at the end of each sentence. Use:

3 periods (.)   1 exclamation point (!)   1 question mark (?)

> Pele was poor   He did not have shoes   He did not have a soccer ball   How did Pele play soccer without shoes or a ball   Pele played in his bare feet with a ball made out of a stuffed sock

Now write two sentences of your own. One of your sentences should need an exclamation point.

_____

_____

_____

Horse Race

Exclamation points go at the ends of some sentences. People use them to show excitement. Which sentence would you end with an exclamation point?

a. I am sleepy   **b. I made my first goal**

Correct the sentences by putting a mark at the end of each sentence. Use:

5 periods (.)   1 exclamation point (!)   1 question mark (?)

Yesterday I was happy   Why was I happy   I played soccer   I ran up and down the field   The score was even   Then, I got the ball   I made my first goal

Imagine you are a racehorse. Write about a race you were in. Use the word **I** because you are writing as if you were the horse. Write at least one sentence that needs an exclamation point.

_____

_____

_____

_____

Come See Sue!

You go to a museum. It is a science museum. Why do you want to go to a science museum? You saw a poster. The poster made you excited. The poster made you want to go see the exhibit. The poster had a big line. The line said, "Come See Sue!"

> ## Sue
>
> What—largest T. Rex skeleton in the world
>
> Where—at the Field Museum in Chicago
>
> When—open every day but Christmas from 9:00 to 5:00

Make a poster for Sue. Include the information about **what**, **where**, and **when**. Include lines to excite people. Use exclamation points on the exciting lines. Decorate your poster.

Come See Sue!

_____

_____

_____

_____

_____

Think of something you would like to star in. It could be a game, a movie, a circus, a play, or a television show.

Make a poster for the event. In your poster, include information about **what, where,** and **when**. Include lines to excite people. Use exclamation points on the exciting lines.

The Climbing Man

Erik was blind. Erik said, "I can climb."

Erik climbed Mt. Everest. How did he do it? Erik did not give up.
Erik didn't give up. He followed the sound of bells. The bells were
tied to other climbers.

◆◆◆◆◆◆◆◆◆◆◆◆◆◆◆◆◆◆

Write down the words that are different in these two sentences:

1. **Erik did not give up.**   2. **Erik didn't give up.**

_____   _____

When you write, you can use **did not** or **didn't**. They mean the
same thing. Which one should you use? It is up to you! You can
use both! Think about what sounds best for your story.

Write about a time you did not stop or didn't give up doing or
learning something. Use the words **did not** and **didn't**.

_____

_____

_____

_____

The Biggest

Finish the conversation between Brian and Frannie. Make sure Frannie says the words **did not** and **didn't**.

Brian: A cat is big.

Frannie: You *didn't* say the biggest thing. What is bigger?

Brian: A dog is big.

Frannie: You *did not* say the biggest thing. Say what is bigger.

Brian: _____

_____

Fannie: _____

_____

Brian: _____

_____

Frannie: _____

_____

Brian: _____

_____

Not Hot

What is not hot? Ice is not hot.

What isn't hot? Ice isn't hot.

Write down the words that are different in these two sentences.

1. What is not hot?   2. What isn't hot?

_____   _____

When you write, you can use **is not** or **isn't**. They mean the same thing. Which one should you use? It is up to you! You can use both! Think about what sounds best for your story.

Write the answers to the questions in complete sentences. Use **is not** or **isn't**.

What is not big? _____

_____

What isn't old? _____

_____

What isn't fast? _____

_____

Blue Polar Bear

Finish the conversation between May and Matt. Make sure Matt says the words **is not** and **isn't**. You can use the Word Bank below for ideas.

May: A polar bear is blue.

Matt: No, it is not. A polar bear is white.

May: A zebra is red and green.

Matt: _____

May: _____

Matt: _____

May: _____

Matt: _____

May: _____

Matt: _____

Word Bank						
cat	dog	horse	turtle	frog	mouse	tiger
orange	pink	yellow	green	brown	black	white

When you write, you need to check your spelling. If you spell words correctly, then the reader knows what you mean.

Weird is a hard word to spell. It is in a list. It is in a list of words that are most often spelled wrong.

When something is weird, it is strange. It is odd.

Correct the spelling in the following sentences:

A wierd thing about butterflies is that they taste with their feet.

It may seem wierd, but a snake uses its tongue to smell.

Write one or two sentences of your own with the word **weird**. You get to pick what you think is weird. When you are done writing, make sure you go back and check your spelling.

_____

_____

_____

_____

A Weird Sight

Imagine you are walking. You see something very weird. Write a letter to your friend. In it, tell all about the weird thing you saw.

Did you see an animal, a monster, or someone doing something very strange? Use the word **weird** in your letter. When you are done, make sure you go back and check your spelling.

Dear _____ ,

Today when I was walking, _____

_____

_____

_____

_____

_____

_____

_____ ,

_____

All About Bones

Circle each phrase that is correct.

1. **It is**   **It are**

2. **They is**   **They are**

> Is and **are** are forms of the verb **to be**.
> **Is** goes with **it**, **he**, and **she**.
> **Are** goes with **you**, **they,** and **we**.

Correct the sentences by making sure the subject has the right verb form (6 changes).

> How many bones is there in an adult? There is 206 bones in an adult. One bone are the longest. It are in the leg. Three bones is the smallest. They is in the ear.

Use the information to write a sentence or two:
A child has 300 bones. As a child grows, some of the bones join together.

Tell if you have more or fewer bones than your teacher. Tell why. When you are done, read over your work. You can use any verb you want, but check that your verb form agrees with your subject.

_____

_____

_____

_____

Seven and Seven

Circle each sentence that is correct.

1.   A giraffe has a neck.   A giraffe have a neck.

2.   Children has necks.   Children have necks.

Has and **have** are forms of the verb **to have**.

Has goes with **it, he,** and **she.**

Have goes with **you, they,** and **we.**

Correct the sentences by making sure the subject has the right form of the verb **to have** or **to be** (5 changes).

A giraffe have seven bones in its neck. How many bones do children has in their necks? Children has seven bones. Why are a giraffe's neck longer? The giraffe's bones is bigger.

Imagine a giraffe is showing off. The giraffe is showing off because it says it has more bones in its neck.

Write down what the giraffe needs to learn. When you are done, read over your work. Make sure your verb forms agree with your subjects.

_____

_____

_____

What Goes with Ant?

An ant ate an apple.

Write the word from the sentence above that went in front of **ant** and **apple**.

_____ ant _____ apple

When do we use **an**? When do we use **a**?
We put **an** in front of words that start with a vowel.

Vowels: A   E   I   O   U

Fix the sentences below by making sure **a** and **an** are used correctly (7 changes).

> A ant is a insect. A ant will eat an banana. A ant will eat an cookie and a apple.

Write a sentence or two about an aunt. Tell if an aunt and an ant are the same. Is an aunt a man or a woman? Do you have an aunt?

_____

_____

_____

Read over your work. Did you use **a** and **an** correctly?

The Visiting Aunt

Imagine you have an aunt who is coming to visit. Give your aunt a name.

Imagine that your aunt has an orange and a banana for breakfast. Write about what your aunt eats for breakfast. Then tell what you and your aunt do for the rest of the day.

This is your story—imagine doing anything you want!

_____

_____

_____

_____

_____

_____

_____

Now that you are done, read over your work. Did you use **a** and **an** correctly in front of **orange** and **banana**? How about in the rest of the story?

Initials

Your initials are the first letters of your name. After initials, you put periods.

> ### Example
> Robert Louis Stevenson is R. L. Stevenson, or R. L. S.

Write your name using initials like in the example:

_____

Think of a name. It could be of a real person or made up. Write down the full name, and then write it using initials for the first and middle name.

_____

_____

Now pretend that this person is coming to dinner. Tell what you will feed your guest. Name your guest using initials for the last name also.

_____ **is coming to dinner.**

_____

_____

Go back and check your work. Did you remember to put a period after each initial?

Writing Prompts

Prompt 1

There is a race. The race is up the Empire State Building! The race is up 86 flights of stairs. This is 1,576 stairs! How could you get ready for such a race?

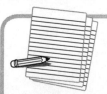

Prompt 2

Long ago, elephants had short noses. They did not have long trunks. This changed when . . .

Prompt 3

One time, I was very hot. When was I hot? Why was I hot? How did I cool down?

Prompt 4

One morning, I heard a sound in my closet. The sound was . . .

Prompt 5

Owen brought his pet snake to class. The snake was in a cage. Owen put the cage behind the teacher's desk to keep it safe. When it was Show-and-Tell time, Owen went to get his snake. The cage was empty!

Prompt 6

How is Saturday different from Monday? Do you do the same things on Saturdays and Mondays?

Prompt 7

One morning there was a knock on my bedroom door. The knocking wouldn't stop. Finally, I got out of bed. I opened the door, and there was a dinosaur! The dinosaur said, "Good morning. May I please come in?" I . . .

Prompt 8

One man was over eight feet tall. Would it be easy or hard to be eight feet tall? Name at least one good thing and one bad thing about being eight feet tall.

Prompt 9

One day I was swimming in the sea. Suddenly I felt something bump me under the water. It was a dolphin!

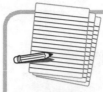

Prompt 10

Imagine you are a tree. You pick what kind. Does anyone climb or make a home in your branches? Do you have fruit that people or animals eat?

Prompt 11

Where have you spent a night other than your own room? Was it at a friend's or relative's house? Was it camping? What did you do?

Prompt 12

You take a bite of a magic cookie. Suddenly, you feel yourself shrinking! You shrink and shrink. You do not stop shrinking until you are only six inches tall! What do you do? Is it fun or hard to be six inches tall? What are some things you can do and can't do when you are very small?

Prompt 13

The bravest person I know is . . .

Prompt 14

You are on your bike. You pedal as fast as you can. Suddenly, your bike starts to go up! You are flying! Tell what happens next.

Prompt 15

How many teeth have you lost? What happened when you lost your teeth?

Prompt 16

A rabbit wanted to get across the river. A crocodile said, "Get in my mouth. I will carry you across." What should the rabbit do? Why?

Prompt 17

One morning I got up and looked in the mirror. I couldn't see myself! I had turned invisible. I was going to be invisible for one whole day. I had to make my day an adventure. First, I . . .

Prompt 18

Being kind is important. Tell about a time when someone was kind to you or you were kind to someone else. How did you feel?

Prompt 19

You are planning a meal for a prince or princess. What will you serve him or her to eat and drink?

Prompt 20

Some people eat with their fingers. Other people use chopsticks or silverware. What do you use? What is a good thing about the way you eat?

Prompt 21

Your whole family is going on a trip. You get to pick where! Where will you go? How will you get there? What will you do?

Prompt 22

You find a box. You open it up. What does the box look like? Is it big or little? What is in it?

Prompt 23

A zebra asks you, "Do I look okay?" The zebra does not have black and white stripes. It has blue and orange polka dots! What do you say?

Prompt 24

Mercury is a planet. It was named after the Roman god Mercury. He could go very fast. He was a messenger god. The planet Mercury moves fast across the sky, so that is why it was called Mercury. You discover a new planet. You get to name it. What will you call your planet? Why?

Prompt 25

Describe your favorite outfit or thing to wear. Describe what it is, the colors, and who gave it to you or where you got it.

Prompt 26

There is a big storm. A big tree is knocked over by the wind. The tree hits the electric wires, and suddenly, the house goes dark!

Prompt 27

You are writing a letter to the president. In your letter, you will ask him some questions. What will you ask the president?

Prompt 28

You feel a tap on your shoulder. You turn around and, much to your surprise, you . . .

Prompt 29

"Run!" your best friend shouted. "We have to run fast if we want to get away!" You . . .

Prompt 30

Describe a relative. What does this relative look like? How are you related? What does he or she do? What have you done with your relative?

Prompt 31

The phone is ringing. Your mom answers it. Then she hands the phone to you with a puzzled look on her face. She says, "The phone is for you. It is the keeper at the zoo. Why is the zoo keeper calling you?"

Prompt 32

You put a message in a bottle. Then you throw the bottle out in the water. What will your message say?

Prompt 33

You are a captain! Would you rather be the captain of a ship or a plane? Give one reason why.

Prompt 34

What kind of animal flies and sits on its eggs? What would happen if you sat on its eggs? Why?

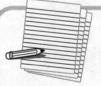

Prompt 35

How are you different from a rhinoceros?

Prompt 36

It is backwards day! You meet your friend. You say, "Goodbye." After you and your friend play on the swings, you leave. When you leave, you say, "Hello."

On backwards day, when might you say, "That's good" or "That's not good?" When might you laugh or say, "Ouch!"